Why Europe?

JØRGEN MØLLER

Why Europe?

AARHUS UNIVERSITY PRESS

Contents

Foreword

For around a decade and a half, I have been trying to wrap my head around European state formation. In 2015, I published a small reflection (*Tænkepause*) titled *Europe* with Aarhus University Press, which argued that the modern Europe we know has deep historical roots. The book said more specifically that developments in medieval Europe had created a combination of external and internal pressure on state-builders, which set the backdrop for the much later development of the modern bureaucratic state, modern representative democracy, and the modern market economy. In 2022, I published a book with Oxford University Press (co-authored with Jonathan Stavnskær Doucette) that further developed these ideas. My 2015 book had begun with the famous confrontation between Pope Gregory VII and German Emperor Henry IV at the castle of Canossa in Tuscany in January 1077. In the 2022 book, *The Catholic Church and European State-Formation*, Jonathan and I set out to show how the ensuing "conflict of church and state"[1] had shaped European state formation, more precisely the development of the multistate system and the ascendancy of strong social groups (clergy, nobility, and townsmen) that could balance monarchs. The 2022 book carefully applied these ideas empirically; it included a lot of statistical analysis that is probably impenetrable to outsiders. Indeed, reviews of the book showed that even trained historians found these analyses difficult to follow.

This book therefore tries a more catholic approach, if you will excuse the term. It gathers fifteen years of thoughts on European state formation into a much more accessible historical narrative. The book is addressed to a wider audience than my previous research on the topic. My hope is that it will be read by the historically minded lay reader but also that it will be of interest to scholars working on the subject in neighbouring disciplines such as history, archaeology, anthropology, and sociology. I have relegated all references to endnotes in order to create a free-flowing narrative.

The title is a daring one as it addresses the very question that first prompted modern social science: *Why Europe?* What made Western and Central Europe, long an economic and political backwater compared with the other great agrarian civilisations of Eurasia, the cradle of modernity? This short book does not, of course, provide a conclusive answer, nor does it describe the long and twisted road that led to modern-day Europe. But the attempt is still bold: to give the reader a sense of the deep roots of European state formation using a hopefully entertaining historical narrative set at a brisk pace.

History writing is being affected by generative artificial intelligence, meaning that readers cannot know in advance what portion of a narrative text has been produced through automated text-generation systems and what has been written by the author. So, full disclosure: this book is written in the old-fashioned style. I have not used AI for anything; the words are my own, as are the thoughts behind them, and the books that are referenced have been painstakingly read under the evening lamp, cover to cover. Time will tell if this short book is a swansong for that manual way of writing history; in the meantime, I hope the readers will appreciate the efforts taken. Throughout the text, I have deliberately used a string of old-fashioned terms to reflect the historical context the book deals with. I have taken the liberty of paraphrasing a couple of sections from my 2015 *Tænkepause* on Europe. This shows how the threads connect this book, written at the end of a long research process, with that one, which was written as a first broad attempt to grapple with the same subject more than a decade ago. I also draw extensively on my collaborative work with Jonathan Stavnskær Doucette, without whom my research agenda on the Catholic Church and European state formation could not have been realised. I would like to thank an anonymous reviewer for reading and commenting on an earlier version of the manuscript and the Aarhus University Research Foundation for financial support. I am also grateful to Henrik Jensen and Karina Bell Ottosen at Aarhus University Press for encouragement, comments, and assistance.

This short book is dedicated to the memory of Mogens Herman Hansen (1940–2024), who meant so much to me, personally as well as professionally.

The Claim 1

The Medieval Rubbish

Karl Marx famously referred to the French Revolution as a 'gigantic broom' that swept away 'all manner of medieval rubbish'.[2] Marx here echoed the negative image of the Middle Ages that dominated the Renaissance and the Enlightenment. The very word "Renaissance" signifies an ambition to orchestrate a rebirth or revival of the knowledge of Antiquity whereas the "Middle Ages" refers to the stagnant period between Antiquity and its rebirth. In the fourteenth century, Italian humanist Francesco Petrarca, commonly known as Petrarch in English, had seen himself as placed at the end of a dark and obscure era that would finish when the beacon of Antiquity was set ablaze again. In the ensuing centuries, "medieval" became a byword for misery, superstition, and brutality; an image that has survived in the notion of the *Dark Ages*, popular even today though historians have long since abandoned it.

The premise of this book is that the "medieval rubbish" nurtured the seeds of modern Europe. It did so by creating power pluralism between and within political units. International competition has been identified as the crucial fact of European state formation. Almost a hundred years ago, German historian Otto Hintze emphasised how Europe was created in a context of *Schieben und Drängen* – push and pull.[3] The English idiom about how push comes to shove conveys Hintze's central insight: that international competition constantly incentivised European rulers to augment their administrative, military, and economic capacity. This idea was later picked up by scholars of international relations who described how the balance of power in the international system pressured states to upgrade their capabilities for warfare.[4]

But European state formation also saw a second balancing act: between rulers and elite groups. Monarchs confronted a society of orders[5] in the form of nobles, clergy, and townsmen. The British philosopher Ernest Gellner saw these groups as the harbingers of the civil societies that came to characterise Western and Central Europe and which at one and the same time balance state power and undergird it.[6] Long before that, French philosopher Montesquieu had argued that it was the nobility that, by acting as a counterweight against monarchs, had created the Western tradition of liberty – an argument picked up by his compatriot Alexis de Tocqueville, who used it to sketch the path that led to the French Revolution.[7]

This double balancing act has long been seen as a necessary condition for the modernisation process that in recent centuries has culminated in the modern state, the modern market economy, and modern democracy: the trinity that nineteenth- and early twentieth-century sociologists attempted to explain.[8] This enterprise – which sparked modern social science – has been coined as an attempt to answer the question 'Why Europe?'[9]

Why did the breakthrough to the modern world occur in this hitherto remote corner of Eurasia, which by AD 1000 seemed to have such poor prospects?[10] What are the historical roots of the "great divergence"[11] that after the Industrial Revolution and the American and French Revolutions would make European societies and their colonial offshoots leap away from the other great agrarian civilisations of Eurasia?

More than a hundred years ago, German sociologist Max Weber referred to this as the "old question", and it would certainly be pretentious, perhaps even preposterous, to claim that this book provides a final answer. The aim is more modest: to show that this development has deep historical roots and thus cannot be ascribed to the Reformation, the Renaissance, the Enlightenment, or Industrialisation. Likewise, it does not – in the main – owe to the legacy from Ancient Greece and Ancient Rome.[12] The crucial juncture occurred in backward medieval Europe, in a society that was strikingly poor and undeveloped compared with the much more prosperous areas in the Middle East, India, and China.

Enter the Catholic Church

More precisely, the claim of this book is that we cannot understand the rise of modern Europe without factoring in the power pluralism sparked by the eleventh-century conflict between the Catholic Church and European lay rulers. This 'Papal Revolution', as American legal scholar Harold J. Berman termed

Max Weber (1864–1920)
The German sociologist Max Weber devoted much of his career to answering the "Why Europe?" question, which he allegedly himself described as the 'old question'. Weber emphasized the importance of the medieval European "free cities", as well as the role played by Christianity in general and the Protestant Reformation in particular. This photograph of Weber was taken in 1918, at 54 years old, two years before his untimely death in Munich in 1920.

it,[13] has been the subject of a flurry of recent books by political scientists.[14] As this literature stresses – and as pointed out by the aforementioned Otto Hintze in an unpublished essay dating to 1931[15] – the eleventh-century rupture meant that European emperors, kings, and princes henceforth had to tread a fine line: caught between the opposition they encountered from strong social groups such as townsmen, nobles, and Catholic clergy and from other European rulers.[16]

These developments, sparked by the Papal Church, were crucial for European state formation. They fatally weakened the authority of what was the strongest political unit a millennium ago, the Holy Roman Empire.[17] Europe was never again to be ruled by a single political entity that claimed a higher authority than all other units. All attempts – from the Salian and Hohenstaufen Emperors in the eleventh, twelfth, and thirteenth centuries, to the Habsburg Charles V and Philip II in the sixteenth century, to the Bourbon Louis XIV in the seventeenth century, and to Napoleon and Hitler closer to our own time – ultimately failed. Instead, Europe became a conglomerate of competing territorial states, which constantly pressured each other politically as well as economically.

As pointed out by Austrian historian Walter Scheidel in the aptly titled book *Escape From Rome*,[18] this absence of empire made Europe differ from all the other great agrarian civilisations of Eurasia, located in the Middle East, India, and East Asia. In these areas, empire had much more staying power, even if we also find periods of fragmentation. For instance, the centuries-long Chinese Warring States Period, which has been likened to the later European system of territorial states, was brought to a swift end in 221 BC when the strongest state – Qin, the source of the modern word "China" – conquered all its competitors.[19] A couple of centuries earlier, the area that is today northern China had housed well over a hundred political units. The generalised geopolitical pressure of the Warring States Period reduced these to a mere seven heavily armed fighting machines; when the dominoes fell in 221 BC, only one was left standing. Afterwards, China experienced periods of prolonged imperial stability interspersed with periods where the great realm was divided, but it never saw a fall-back to a genuine multistate system. According to calculations by political scientists Mark Dincecco and Yuhua Wang, in the period 1000–1799, the Chinese area contained an average of 1.5 states; Europe an average of 85 states.[20]

The failure of empire is thus the crucial fact about medieval and early modern Europe. The result was that European monarchs were constrained, internationally and domestically. They not only faced off against each other, they were also balanced internally by strong nobles, a strong clergy, and – after the twelfth-century commercial revolution – vibrant towns. European emperors, kings, and princes constantly had to walk the tightrope, and if they fell off it, they would face dire consequences in the form of external defeat or internal rebellion.

European Restlessness

The tension between lay and religious authority regularly produced crises and upheavals. From a world-historical perspective, we can view this as both the great failure and the great success of European state formation. It was a failure in that the Latin West never created the kind of stable social order prized by political theorists throughout written history, the stability that characterised, say, the Ancient Egypt of the Pharaohs or the Chinese Han Empire.[21]

Most contemporaries saw only the sign of the devil in the many upheavals and instability that characterised European affairs, and they longed for the firmness and constancy celebrated by conservatives everywhere. This was, after all, a society where the best defence of any action was that this was the way things had always been done – even law was found, not made, as the saying goes. But over time, the very instability and lability that intellectuals decried proved the source of great dynamism. It gave birth to the "rational restlessness" that Max Weber spent most of his career investigating: the relentless search for more effective administrative, military, economic, and political models and designs. As British political scientist Samuel P. Finer puts it in his magisterial three-volume work, *The History of Government*, 'Europe was always travelling but never arrived'.[22]

To understand why, let us start by going back to a historical character who is closely associated with today's European project in the form of EU integration. Since 1950, he has lent his name to a prestigious yearly prize that the German city of Aachen awards for work done in the service of European unification. Since 2007, the British magazine *The Economist*'s weekly column on European politics has borne his name. For it is with Charlemagne that our story commences.

The Rupture 2

Making an Emperor

It all began in the Eternal City. Not the splendid metropolis of the august emperors of Antiquity but the ruined Rome of the early medieval popes.[23] On Christmas Day, AD 800, Charles, King of the Franks and Lombards, was crowned Emperor of the Romans by Pope Leo III in the Old St Peter's Basilica. When the sun set on the Tiber that evening, Leo and Charles had founded a Western imperial line, rivalling the one in the Byzantine Empire, which traced itself back to Caesar and Augustus. They had, thereby, established the axis – papacy at one pole and empire at the other – around which the destiny of medieval Europe would turn.

Charles is one of the few individuals in history to have greatness built into his name. He is known to posterity as "Charlemagne", Charles the Great. But he was not so great that he could simply proclaim himself emperor as another French ruler, Napoleon Bonaparte, was to do a thousand years later; he needed the assistance of the pope. By placing the imperial crown on Charles's head, creating the first emperor of the Latin West since the demise of the Western Roman Empire in the fifth century, Leo III bequeathed to his papal successors a mighty weapon: the power to refuse a would-be emperor his crown or, possibly, take it away from one already crowned.[24] This, in turn, meant that emperors had a keen interest in having friendly popes elected, preferably making them subservient to the empire.

The resulting tension between religious and secular authority would echo down the centuries. In the words of English historian of ideas Francis Oakley, it created a society characterised 'by a deeply institutional dualism and racked by the internal instability resulting there from'.[25] This dualism was to be the motor of European state formation, at least throughout the high and late Middle Ages, which makes up one of the turning points of history, according to this book.

We can think of this sundering of religious and lay power as a rupture that did away with the normal way of organising agrarian civilisations: sacral monarchy, or what Oakley has termed 'the theopolitical commonsense of humankind'.[26] The king-as-priest (occasionally the priest-as-king) has characterised most historical societies, as Ernest Gellner has emphasised.[27] The Chinese emperor with his celestial mandate; the Islamic Caliph, successor to the prophet, Muhammed; and the Byzantine emperor, claiming the mantle of Constantine the Great, the first Christian emperor, all exemplify this social order, which fused lay and religious authority, creating a sacral state presided over by a holy monarch.[28] But in Western and Central Europe, the priest (pope) and the king (emperor) faced each other. As American historian Brian Tierney long ago pointed out, we find numerous other agrarian civilisations

The Arch of Constantine
Before the famous Battle of the Milvian Bridge, fought outside Rome in October 312, the Roman emperor Constantine reportedly experienced a dream or vision in which he was instructed to fight – and prevail – under a Christian symbol. Constantine would become the first Roman emperor to support the new religion and perhaps even to convert to it on his deathbed. He was also responsible for convening the first ecumenical church councils, including the renowned Council of Nicaea in 325, at which the original version of the Church's creed – hence known as the Nicene Creed – was formulated. The picture shows the Arch of Constantine, as seen from the south side, erected to commemorate his victory at the Milvian Bridge and located in Rome near the Colosseum.

than the European – but none in which religious and lay power engaged in a similar arm-wrestling contest.[29]

Henry and Gregory at Canossa

The most famous example of the tension between religious and lay authority is the clash between Pope Gregory VII (r. 1073–1085) and emperor-elect and King of Germany, Italy, and Burgundy Henry IV (r. 1054–1105), which broke out in earnest in 1076.[30] At his Lent synod in Rome that year, Gregory excommunicated and deposed Henry. In response, Henry declared the 'false monk'[31] Hildebrand (Gregory's name before his papal election in 1073) deposed at a council of German bishops.

King Henry soon found that he had overplayed his hand. He had long faced an internal rebellion, the epicentre of which was the northern region of Saxony but which by 1076 had come to march under the banner of Henry's former liegeman Rudolf of Swabia. The conflict with Gregory strengthened the rebels' hand, and an increasingly desperate Henry was forced to seek a reconciliation with the pope. This was the backdrop of King Henry's notorious Walk to Canossa in January 1077.

Watching the fire that his excommunication and deposition of Henry had kindled, Gregory moved out from Rome and went north. His plan was to cross the Alps and hold a synod in Germany where he would deal with the imperial crisis. But Henry moved faster. Crossing the Alps in the opposite direction, on 25 January, he intercepted Gregory at the Tuscan Castle of Canossa, owned by Countess Mathilde, the ruler of the

March of Tuscany and a staunch ally of the pope. Wearing the garments of a penitent, Henry prostrated himself at Canossa's gate for three days, begging the pope to forgive him.

Gregory, attended by Mathilde and his friend and confidant Abbot Hugh of Cluny, who also happened to be Henry's godfather, pondered how to react. Perhaps egged on by the conciliatory Hugh, perhaps genuinely moved by Henry's apparent remorse and penitence and his long-standing respect for the young king's deceased father, Emperor Henry III, Gregory finally relented. Henry was let into the castle where he took communion with the pope, who annulled the excommunication.

Henry's walk to Canossa has imprinted itself into the collective memory of Europeans. *Nach Canossa gehen wir nicht*, we shall not walk to Canossa, German Chancellor Otto von Bismarck said in the German Bundestag in 1872 when defending his attempt to secularise parts of German education presided over by the Catholic Church. In my own native Danish, *Canossagang*, walking to Canossa, means demeaning oneself or asking for penitence; Italians use *L'umiliazione di Canossa*, the humiliation at Canossa.

However, the drama at Canossa did not mark the end of the story about Henry and Gregory. The pope soon learned that the emperor-elect had not mended his ways, and three years later, Henry was again excommunicated by Gregory, who in March 1080 went so far as to recognise Rudolf of Swabia as the legitimate German king.

This time, Henry managed to turn the tables on his opponents. Rudolf of Swabia routed the Salian forces in October

1080 at the Battle of Elster but was mortally wounded in the fray – losing his right hand and taking a sword stab in the belly – and he died the next day at Merseburg. After this stroke of luck, Henry went on the offensive, engaging in the traditional *expeditio Italica*, "Italian expedition",[32] of medieval German emperors. In 1082 and in 1083, he besieged Rome and ravaged much of northern and central Italy, including Mathilde's Tuscan lands. Easter 1084 found Gregory holed up in the impregnable Castel Sant'Angelo, originally built by Roman Emperor Hadrian as a mausoleum, now a refuge of last resort for beleaguered popes.

Only by calling to his aid the Norman duke, Robert Guiscard, the ruler of much of southern Italy, did Gregory force Henry to retreat. But the pope got more than he bargained for: Guiscard's Norman host sacked several Roman neighbourhoods, and an unpopular Gregory had to retreat with them to Salerno, where he died in May 1085. Allegedly, his dying words, memorialised on his sarcophagus – a paraphrase of Psalm 44:8 in the Old

Henry's Walk to Canossa

At the heart of the Investiture Controversy lay the question of who held the right to appoint bishops and abbots – the secular rulers (emperors, kings, and princes) or the community of believers, represented by the Church. The conflict came to a head in 1076, when Pope Gregory VII excommunicated and deposed the German king Henry IV. In January 1077, Henry prostrated himself outside the castle of Canossa in Tuscany in an effort to persuade Gregory to rescind the excommunication. According to tradition, Henry stood barefoot in the snow, dressed in penitential garments, for three days while begging the pope for forgiveness. The illustration shows how the German painter Eduard Schwoiser imagined this dramatic scene in 1862.

Testament – were: 'I have loved justice and hated iniquity; therefore, I die in exile'.[33]

The Crusades and the Investiture Controversy

The conflict of church and state did not end with Gregory's death. Henry had set up a rival pope, Clement III, who had crowned him emperor in Rome in 1084, and who controlled Rome until his death in 1100. But Gregory was followed by a line of "Gregorian" popes, first the ineffectual Victor III, who had previously been abbot of the great monastery of Montecassino, then the competent Urban II, Hugh of Cluny's former second-in-command and close associate of Gregory VII after he moved to Rome to become cardinal-bishop of Ostia around 1080.

Barred from Rome by the imperial antipope, Urban, who was elected pope in 1088, leveraged the Gregorian ideas to fortify his position. His masterstroke was to call the First Crusade at the Council of Clermont in southern France in November 1095.[34] Urban's call sparked mass enthusiasm and recruitment across what is today southern and central France. The foolhardy expedition that followed was successful against all odds, conquering Jerusalem in 1099 and establishing a series of Latin enclaves in Syria and Palestine, including the Kingdom of Jerusalem.

The First Crusade was a gory enterprise that culminated in the wholesale slaughter of the Muslim and Jewish population of Jerusalem. Crusading turned prior Christian teachings on their head. Where violence had hitherto been seen as demanding penitence – even when it was just, according to the criteria stipulated by Augustine – crusade violence now came to be seen as a penitential act, what British historian Christopher Tyerman refers to as the 'Christianisation of war'.[35] This spectacular volte-face was, in the eyes of contemporaries, vindicated by the result, the conquest of the holy of holies, the Church of the Holy Sepulchre in Jerusalem. As the eminent historian of the crusades Jonathan Riley-Smith notes, '[i]f the First Crusade had failed there can be little doubt that senior churchmen would have arisen out of the shadows to condemn it, but with its triumph doubts of penitential warfare evaporated'.[36]

Urban did not live to see this; he died before the news of the conquest of Jerusalem reached him. But due to the spectacular success of the First Crusade, the Gregorian party won the contest over the hearts and mind – or at least the allegiance – of the churchmen of Latin Christendom.[37] In the words of Tyerman, from as early as 1100, 'the cause of Jerusalem transcended the political divide of the Investiture Contest, in posthumous tribute to Urban II's triumph'.[38]

This development was to cost Henry IV the throne he had fought so tenaciously against Gregory to keep. While the emperor did not set up another antipope after the death of Clement III in 1100, he still refused to come to terms with the Gregorian party. This created an intolerable situation, and on the last day of the year in 1105, Henry's son and namesake, Henry V, forced his father to abdicate with the intention of brokering a compromise with Rome.

To understand Henry V's conciliatory overtones, we need to say a bit more about what was at stake in the conflict between pope and emperor, or between the papacy and lay monarchs more generally. The conflict between Gregory and Henry IV was a consequence of the tenth-century church reform movement, which I describe in detail in the next chapter. But its trigger was that the pope and the young emperor-elect found themselves fighting over the appointment of the archbishop of one of the wealthiest and mightiest sees (bishoprics) in Europe: Milan in northern Italy.[39]

Gregory maintained that the Milanese archbishop – heir to the great St Ambrose, one of the four doctors of the Catholic Church, the others being St Jerome, St Augustine, and St Gregory the Great – should be elected by the community of believers and that the pope had the right to act as umpire; Henry upheld the imperial, or royal, right of investiture, which had been practised at Milan for centuries. The result was a falling out: the emperor-elect appointed one archbishop, Gregory sponsored another.[40]

It was against this background that Gregory in 1075 set down in writing the so-called *Dictatus Papae*, 27 dictations or notes entered into the papal register. The *Dictatus* does not seem to have been intended as a formal declaration of papal prerogatives, but it sheds light on Gregory's personal view of the relationship between lay and religious authority, which guided his papal policies.[41] In the most famous of the clauses, Gregory declared that '[i]t may be permitted to him to depose emperors'. It was this power he invoked the next year at his Lent synod to depose Henry IV. In other clauses, Gregory claimed the right to invest bishops and other clergymen with their offices and to depose, reinstate, or transfer them at will.

This last set of prerogatives came to dominate the conflict of church and state. Lay monarchs could not well relinquish their control of investiture – particularly of bishops but also of abbots and other high church offices – if they wanted to rule their realms. At this point in time, one of the few royal prerogatives left to the weak Capetian monarchs of France was the right to appoint bishops across large swathes of northern France. In the Holy Roman Empire, the bishops in many ways made up the most important part of the imperial power infrastructure.[42]

Royally appointed bishops controlled land, wealth, and men-at-arms, and they served as the local agents of the monarchs that had raised them to their high station. To increase royal control, Henry III and Henry IV had deliberately attempted to strengthen the German bishops at the expense of their unruly and combative nobility. Losing their sway over clerical appointments would mean forfeiting their most important source of patronage, and it would sever the clerical arm of royal government, what German historians term the *Reichskirchensystem*.[43]

Once it was clear that the Gregorian line had been victorious within the church hierarchy, lay monarchs felt compelled to come to an understanding with Rome. Compromises were brokered with the English and French kings in 1107, and Henry V attempted to achieve a similar rapprochement for the empire. However, as more was at stake, the negotiations were protracted and difficult. Only in 1122 – at the Concordat of Worms, named after the German town in which it was concluded – was a final agreement between pope and emperor reached.

This took the form of a compromise where bishops were required to swear allegiance to the lay monarch, but the selection itself was left to the church, which also formally invested the bishop with ring and staff. Strong monarchs could use this veto to *de facto* appoint bishops. A good illustration comes from England, perhaps the realm of the Latin West with the highest state capacity at the time, where in 1173 King Henry II sent the following – blunt and laconic – instructions to the churchmen who were to elect the new bishop of Winchester, one of the central sees in the kingdom: 'I order you to hold a free election but forbid you to elect anyone save Richard, my clerk.'[44]

Likewise, in the German core of the Holy Roman Empire, the emperors retained a veto over episcopal appointments.

The Concordat of Worms, 1122
The Investiture Controversy was formally brought to an end in 1122, when the emperor and the pope reached a compromise known as the Concordat of Worms, named after the town where the agreement was concluded. Similar arrangements had already been made with the English and French kings in 1107. The agreement, negotiated between Pope Callixtus II and Emperor Henry V, is illustrated in this stained glass window from the German city of Mainz, which depicts the pope and the emperor standing together.

WORMSER
KONKORDAT
1122

But where royal power was weaker, monarchs effectively lost control of bishops. South of the Alps, in the rich lands of northern Italy, the German emperors forfeited their authority of intervention when sees appointed new bishops. Finally, the German emperors renounced their right to appoint popes.

The Concordat of Worms thus gave the Holy Roman Emperor important concessions, especially when set alongside Gregory's uncompromising statements in the *Dictatus*. But at the same time, it marked an end of the kind of sacral monarchy that had characterised Europe before what was to become known as the Investiture Controversy. The Concordat of Worms and the similar arrangements made with the English and French monarchs in 1107 established that monarchs – the emperor included – were laymen, not some sort of super-priests.[45] The agreements left many other questions unanswered, and their inconclusive nature meant that the conflict over investiture would resurface at frequent intervals for the remainder of the Middle Ages; indeed, it came to dominate European politics in the following centuries.[46] As Gillingham and Griffiths put it in a short introduction to the subject of medieval England: 'In the mid-twelfth century Church-State relations bristled with problems which could be, and normally were, shelved by men of goodwill but which could provide a field-day for men who were determined to quarrel.'[47]

The Backdrop 3

From Bad Popes to Reformers

The conflict between pope and emperor might strike the reader as unsurprising. From history books and historical novels and movies, we are so used to the image of scheming popes back-stabbing and correcting kings and of kings trying to liberate themselves from the pope's yoke that the fallout seems only natural. The very word "Rome" conjures up an image of a distant but still uncomfortably close and mercurial powerhouse that must be held at arm's length but cannot be ignored. The Norwegian national anthem even has a short celebration of how twelfth-century King Sverre 'spoke bluntly against Rome' (*talte Roma midt imod*).

But in a world-historical perspective, the conflict is in fact exceptional, and it did not come about as an automatic response to the crowning of Charlemagne on that winter's day in Rome in AD 800. For more than two centuries, sacral monarchy stood its ground in Western Europe. English medievalist R. W. Southern describes this period as follows:

> The affairs of the church received little direction from Rome. Monasteries and bishoprics were founded, and bishops and abbots were appointed by lay rulers without

> hindrance or objection; councils were summoned by kings; kings and bishops legislated for their local churches about tithes, ordeals, Sunday observance, penance; saints were raised to the altars – all without reference to Rome.[48]

In fact, the moral influence of the papacy hit an all-time low in the centuries preceding the Walk to Canossa. The tenth and early eleventh centuries are known as the era of "bad popes".[49] The beginning of this era of malign "vicars" sitting on St Peter's throne is normally dated to 897, where Pope Stephen VI disinterred the body of his late predecessor and prior rival Pope Formosus and had the corpse found guilty of usurping the see of Rome in a mock trial.

Worse was to follow in the tenth century as the papacy became a pawn for the Counts of Tusculum, as well as other Roman noble families. Several scandalous popes ascended St Peter's throne during a period that is sometimes referred to as the "pornocracy" (rule of prostitutes) of the papacy. Take, for instance, Pope John XII (r. 955–964), a relative of the Tusculum counts, who according to some sources became pope at the tender age of 18 and who was known for his worldly depravity. The Lateran Palace was spoken of as a brothel during his tenure, and in 964, John was deposed by the first emperor of what came to be known as the Holy Roman Empire: Otto I, the Great.

Things seemed to change for the better in the early tenth century, with several capable and pious popes. But in 1032, another scandalous papacy began. Thanks to bribery, Benedict IX was elected pope despite being only 20 years old. There were persistent rumours linking him to murder and rape, and he was made to step down twice. The first time was in 1044 where the Romans drove him out and elected a new pope named Sylvester III. Benedict managed to stage a comeback the next year but then sold the papacy to his godfather, who took the papal name Gregory VI. There were thus two rival popes, and the tally increased to three when the fickle Benedict changed his mind again and once more claimed the papacy.

At this point, the devout German King Henry III had had enough, and he decided to intervene in Rome. He had a lot of precedence to build on: in less than a hundred years, from Otto the Great's imperial coronation to 1049, the German emperors appointed altogether 12 out of 25 popes.[50] The most assertive German emperor was arguably Otto III whose mother was a byzantine princess (Theophanu) and who in 1098 moved his court to Rome to govern in style as a real Roman emperor. During his time as emperor, Otto III deposed one pope, had another blinded and elevated two non-Italians to St Peter's throne, one of whom was a cousin of his who took the papal name Gregory V (r. 996–999). Indeed, for a hundred years, German kings/emperors 'deposed and appointed more bishops [popes] of Rome than they did the prelates of any other Italian see'.[51]

Acting on this venerable model, in 1046 Henry III convened a synod that deposed all three popes.[52] In their stead, he had a German, Clement II, elevated to the papacy only to see him die the next year. Another imperial appointee, Pope Damasus II, also held out for less than a year. But Henry did not relent, and in 1049, he had his kinsman, Bruno of Egisheim-Dagsburg, elected pope.[53] Bruno strategically insisted that he would only accept becoming St Peter's successor if acclaimed by the Romans themselves, as Pope Leo IX. This gave him street credit in the Eternal City, and he had his back free when he travelled through Germany and France in 1049–50, calling synods to push a new reform agenda, which he had first set out at an Easter synod in Rome in 1049.

The Reform Movement

This reform agenda had two main aims: to eradicate the evils of "simony" and "nicolaitism". Simony was the selling of ecclesiastical offices (for instance, the office of bishop); nicolaitism was clergy marrying or having concubines and thus potentially siring heirs. Both practices entangled the clergy with the lay world and hindered them from following the true Christian path, the *vita religiosa*.[54]

The reform agenda itself can be dated to the half-century before Henry III's intervention in 1046. We normally associate it with the Abbey of Cluny in Bourgogne, which under the two remarkably long abbacies of Odilo (994–1049) and Hugh (1049–1109) – the Hugh who was holed up with Gregory and Mathilde at Canossa in January 1077 – created the first international monastic order, with several hundred daughter houses beholden to the mother house at Cluny and often ruled by abbots sent from here. Via these "Cluniac" monasteries, the reform agenda was spread across much of southern France, northern Spain, western Germany, and northern Italy.[55]

This alliance between laypeople and Cluniacs found expression in the so-called Peace and Truce of God Movement. This was an attempt to pacify a lawless society via religiously backed voluntary oaths made at great church councils. The main purpose of these gatherings was to regulate the rapaciousness of the local noble arms-bearing class, who would prey on both townsmen and peasants, while carrying on their own "private" feuds with each other. For instance, the "truce" of God was a measure that aimed to suspend warfare on religious days, such as during Lent and from Saturday night until Monday evening (later prolonged until Wednesday). The "peace" of God was an even more ambitious undertaking as it was an attempt to outlaw warfare *tout court*: a harbinger of the royal "peace" later promulgated (and sometimes enforced) by medieval kings and princes.[56]

Knock-on effects of the Cluniac programme were felt more directly in many towns as sworn associations of pious townsmen rallied to the reform project by attempting to correct their resident clergy: getting rid of bishops who had paid for their office and clergymen who had wives or concubines.[57] For instance, the conflict between imperially appointed archbishops of the see of St Ambrose and parts of the Milanese population, mentioned above, came about because of to the traction the reform programme had in Milan from the 1040s onwards. It was led by the so-called Patarenes (*patarini*, "ragpickers"[58]), an association of Milanese townsmen who denounced the unreformed local clergy, including their simoniac, imperially appointed archbishops.

The Patarenes forced several archbishops to flee Milan and, in 1073, they managed to take power in the city under a knight named Erlembald. Erlembald was fiercely supported by Pope

Gregory VII, who corresponded regularly with him and proclaimed to the world that he was fighting a holy war, a *bellum Dei*, against those corrupting the church. Erlembald and his Patarenes controlled Milan until 1075 when, having lost goodwill among the Milanese due to a damaging fire, they were defeated by an aristocratic military force allied with Henry IV.[59]

Reconstructed Model of Cluny Abbey
A reconstruction of the third abbey church of the monastery of Cluny, the building of which began in 1088. Around the year 1000, Cluny became a hotbed of a major church reform movement, spreading its ideas via the monastery's numerous daughter houses in France, northern Spain, and northern Italy before finally reaching Rome around 1050, there to metamorphose into what we today call the Gregorian reforms. The third abbey church in Cluny was the largest ecclesiastical building in the Latin West for several centuries; it was sacked and partly destroyed during the French Revolution.

Getting to Rome

But we are getting ahead of our story. With Pope Leo's ascension in 1049, the Cluniac reform agenda was transplanted to Rome where it became official papal policy. At the synods Leo called in Germany and France in 1049–50, he denounced simoniac bishops who had bought their ring and staff and he condemned clerical unchastity, or fornication as it is normally called in older history books.[60]

In this early phase, the papal reform movement did not target the power over churches in the realm of the German emperor; on the contrary, the reforms were carried out in collaboration with Emperor Henry III, who was a pious and devout man according to all sources. But this amicable relationship soured after Henry's death in 1056. His son and heir, Henry IV, began his regal tenure as a child king, something that always weakened royal power.[61] In 1059, an Easter synod called by

The Tripartition of the Frankish Empire at Verdun, 843
The Frankish Empire reached its height under Charlemagne (r. 768–814) and his son Louis the Pious (r. 814–840). Following Louis's death, the empire was divided among his surviving sons. The first such division occurred in 843 with the Treaty of Verdun, as shown on this French historical map. Charles the Bald came to rule the territory that would later become France, Louis the German the lands that would later become Germany, and Lothar I the extensive territory in between, including the wealthy region of northern Italy. Lothar, the eldest son, also inherited the imperial title.

CHARLEMAGNE
émembrement
é de Verdun
843
Explication des Couleurs
rose Royaume de Charles-le-Chauve
vert " de Lothaire
jaune " de Louis-le-Germanique
OCÉAN GERMANIQUE
MER ORIENTALE
MER MÉDITERRANÉE
MER TYRRHÉNIENNE
MER ADRIATIQUE
EAN BRITANNIQUE
NORTHUMBERLAND
DEIRA
GALLES SEPTENTRIONALE
MERCIE
EST-ANGLIE
ESSEX
WESSEX
SUSSEX
KENT
I. de Wight
SCANIE
Danois
I. Bornholm
Poméraniens
Nordalbingiens
Obotrites
Wiltzes
Wélétabes
Léques
Wendes
Peuples Slaves
Sorabes
Tchèques
BOHÊME
MORAVIE
FRISE
SAXE
Angariens
Ostphaliens
Westphaliens
THURINGE
AUSTRASIE
Toxandrie
Brabant
Hesbaye
Fagne
Ardenne
Eifel
Flandre
FRANCE
NEUSTRIE
Maine
Anjou
Nantais
Touraine
Poitou
Berry
Limousin
AQUITAINE
Auvergne
Périgord
Bordelais
Agenais
Quercy
Rouergue
Gévaudan
GASCOGNE
Toulousain
Albigeois
SEPTIMANIE
Narbonnais
Roussillon
MARCHE D'ESPAGNE
Bergedan
Barcelone
Woëvre
LOTHARINGIE
Nordgau
ALSACE
Sundgau
ALLEMAGNE
BAVIÈRE
MARCHE ORIENTALE
(OSTMARK)
MARCHE DE BOHÊME
(NORTHGOWE)
Argovie
Thurgovie
RÉTIE
Alpes
CARINTHIE
CARNIOLE
MARCHE DE FRIOUL
BOURGOGNE
Lyonnais
Genevois
Valais
Val d'Aoste
NEUSTRIE
AUSTRIE
LOMBARDIE
ÉMILIE
Milan
Pavie
PROVENCE
LITTORAL MARITIME
EXARCHAT
PENTAPOLE
TOSCANE
DUCHÉ DE SPOLÈTE
DUCHÉ DE BÉNÉVENT
CORSE
SARDAIGNE
I. d'Elbe
ISTRIE
CROATIE
DALMATIE
SERBIE
Slaves du S
PANNONIE
ROYAUME DES AVARS
Lac Neusiedl

Pope Nicholas II passed an election decree which stated that the cardinal-bishops were henceforth to elect the pope, leaving no say to the Roman population or the German emperor, who had taken turns deciding which candidate was *papabile* in the past.[62]

Around the same time, one of the papal reformers, Cardinal Humbert, issued the tract *Adversus simoniacos* (Against simoniacs). Humbert here broadened the meaning of simony so that it came to include any kind of secular influence on appointments to church offices.[63] Humbert's cardinal idea (pun intended) was that the liberty of the church could only be secured by raising a hard-and-fast barrier against lay influence. This interpretation made imperial investiture of, e.g., bishops an act of simony, even if no direct payment from officeholder to emperor took place.

Humbert was a radical; it was he who in 1054 had unleashed what has come to be known as the Great Schism, or East–West Schism between Latin and Orthodox Christianity. This happened when Humbert, sent as a papal legate to the great city of Constantinople, excommunicated the Byzantine patriarch after a bitter feud, placing the bull (an official order or statement from the pope) on the altar of Hagia Sophia, the great church that Emperor Justinian I had built in Constantinople. Other papal reformers initially resisted Humbert's hard line on simony.[64] But it was his interpretation that ultimately won out, and with Gregory's papacy, it became official policy.[65] As we have seen, Gregory lashed out against *any* lay investiture of bishops, and he encouraged believers to denounce unreformed clergy wherever they were encountered. It was this radical position on investiture that made the conflict with Henry IV all but inevitable.

Revolutions Devour Their Children

These developments illustrate the old saying that revolutions devour their children. Without Henry III's intervention in 1046 and subsequent imperial support of Pope Leo IX, the church reform agenda would not have been transplanted to Rome.[66] Had this not happened, his son Henry IV would not have faced a firebrand pope such as the Gregory, who had accompanied Pope Leo IX when he first travelled to Rome in 1049.

There are several twists to this story. Gregory long sought to avoid a showdown with the son due to his reverence for the father – and the mother, the devout Agnes of Poitou, who had served as the underage Henry's regent until 1061 and had retired to Rome in 1065. Gregory saw it as his responsibility to guide young Henry IV so that he would follow in the pious footsteps of Henry III, and as late as 1075, he still hoped to avoid a break with the king – ultimately in vain as the rupture of 1076 was to show.[67]

Why did the mighty Salian imperial line fail to harness and control the reform agenda they themselves had cultivated? The answer lies in the decentralisation and fragmentation of power that had come to characterise Western Europe in

Hagia Sophia
The Hagia Sophia was built by Byzantine Emperor Justinian I, the Great (r. 527–565) in just five years and 10 months (532–537 CE). It was dedicated to the holy wisdom (Sophia). The great church was henceforth used for imperial coronations in the Byzantine Empire, and as the seat of the Constantinople patriarchate, and it was the most important holy place in the Orthodox Christian World until it was transformed into a mosque (note the four minarets) following the Ottoman conquest in 1453. From 1935–2020, it was a museum, but in 2020 it was reclassified as a mosque.

the two centuries after the death of Charlemagne in 814. Particularly in West Francia, or what became France, royal power had fallen apart. At the nadir of this development, the Capetian kings who replaced the last Carolingian in 987 exercised genuine power only in a small area around Paris.[68]

Southern France was completely out of their remit – no Capetian king set his foot in southern Burgundy until 1166.[69] The Peace and Truce of God Movement can be understood as a bottom-up response to this vacuum of royal power. The same goes for the Cluniac reform movement which spread to the areas where royal power was weakest: southern France, northern Spain, and northern Italy.[70]

It was thus the absence of royal power that made the church reform movement possible in the first place, and it was the very same fragmentation of power that made it so difficult for Henry IV to control the papal reform movement, even after he had chased Gregory VII from Rome.[71] While Henry governed what was by far the strongest polity in the Latin West, he faced trenchant internal opposition, and he was unable to hinder popes such as Gregory from leaning on other rulers, including the Normans of south Italy, or to stop Urban II from harnessing knights across France and Italy to the reform agenda by calling the First Crusade in 1095. Despite his campaign against the "Gregorian" line of popes, Henry never managed to make rulers in, e.g., southern Italy, France, or the Low Countries break with these popes, and he had to watch Urban's triumphal march through northern Italy and France in 1095–96 from the sidelines.

To understand the conflict of church and state, we thus need to factor in the state collapse of the ninth and tenth centuries. English historian Robert Bartlett terms the result of this buckling of royal power the 'fertile confusion of post-Carolingian Europe'.[72] It was this fertile confusion that made it possible for the church reform movement to break centuries of precedence for sacral monarchy.

The Measures 4

The Great Balancer

Joseph Stalin is reputed to have derisively said: 'The Pope? How many divisions has he got?' When we go back to medieval times, the pope would occasionally lead armies into battle but seldom with much success. A case in point is how Leo IX, the first reform pope, led an army against the Normans in southern Italy in 1053, only to suffer an ignominious defeat at the Battle of Civitate on 18 June. That the Norman victors allegedly fell to their knees, begging the captive pope for forgiveness, could not disguise the hard facts: the pope had bet high and lost big, and the Normans would exact their price. Leo was kept in captivity for nine months and forced to ratify treaties that benefited the Normans.

However, the pen is sometimes mightier than the sword. We can well imagine the German pope reflecting on his military failure, shrugging his shoulders, and saying, in medieval German, "*Dann haben wir andere Methoden*" (then we have other measures). The Norman–papal relationship had numerous ups and downs, which reflects the way the reform popes who followed in Leo's wake played the role of balancer. In 1059, six years after the defeat at Civitate, Pope Nicholas II had managed a striking turnaround by allying with the Normans, thenceforth increasingly seen as a counterweight against German imperial power.[73]

Throughout the high and late Middle Ages, popes would continue to play this divide-and-conquer game to ensure that overweening lay power was challenged. This role as the great balancer of European politics began in earnest with the struggle between Gregory VII and Henry IV in the 1070s and 1080s. We have already seen how Gregory ended up supporting Henry's rival, Rudolf of Swabia, blessing the Saxon rebellion against Henry that Rudolf had come to lead.

Closer to home, Gregory benefited from the support the reform movement had already built up among laypeople in much of France and Italy and, to a lesser extent, parts of western Germany. He took advantage of this to get pious townsmen to denounce their simoniac bishops – as in the case of Erlembald and his Patarenes in Milan – and to enlist the support of arms-bearing nobles, known as "the faithful of St Peter" (*fideles beati Petri*), in his struggle against Henry IV.[74] Indeed, from Gregory onwards, the reform papacy came to rely on lay military support to push its religious and political agenda. This culminated in the crusade movement, called by Urban II, and led, among others, by the *fideles beati Petri* Raymond of St Gilles.[75]

But Gregory also worked in a more strategic way centred on peripheral political units in newly Christianised parts of Europe. His relations with rulers in these areas were much more irenic. From the very beginning of his papacy in 1073, Gregory attempted to prop up monarchs on the outskirts of Christian Europe.[76] He did his best to ensure that the Kingdom of Hungary remained independent of the German emperor. In Scandinavia and in England, he encouraged attempts to create strong hereditary kingdoms, preferably with the eldest son inheriting power.[77] As British historian Herbert Edward John Cowdrey summarises:

> Gregory sought to foster among the nations something like a balance of power: more distant peoples were to be established in their independence from outside political supremacy and in the habit of obedience to the papacy; by such means, the power especially of the Salian monarchy in Germany might be kept within bounds.[78]

This is illustrated by Gregory's repeated attempts to groom Danish King Sweyn Estrithson. Sweyn was the only king to whom Gregory, according to his register, sent an official note of his election in 1073, and after Sweyn's death in April 1076, Gregory would posthumously hail him as an ideal Christian ruler (politely overlooking that Sweyn had fathered around twenty children outside of marriage, five of whom were to become kings of Denmark in quick succession). The pope clearly groomed the Danish king as part of his attempt to check German imperial power. Precisely one year before, in April 1075, Gregory had sent Sweyn a letter in which he observed how 'the king of a distant realm, by strong and righteous rule, was to compensate for the unreliability of rulers who were nearer to Rome'.[79] A year and a half later, he blessed the crowning of the Polish King Bolesław II, "the Bold", on Christmas Day

1076, after the king had sided with Gregory in the conflict with Henry.

The heavy-handed papal policy towards Henry IV thus contrasted with the way he dealt with rulers in Poland, Hungary, Scandinavia, and England. Recall that the linchpin of Gregorian reforms was the ban against royal investiture of bishops. Nonetheless, Gregory never attempted to enforce this ban in these outer areas[80] – it was only in the core regions of the Latin West, Germany, France, and Italy, that he took on royal power.[81]

A King is Emperor in His Own Realm

This external balancing act became a cornerstone of papal policy throughout the Middle Ages. Up until the late thirteenth century, German imperial power remained the crucial adversary that popes attempted to contain. The main doctrinal manifestation of the long and ardent papal campaign against the Holy Roman Empire was the way the papacy helped formulate and spread a particular maxim: *Rex in regno suo imperator*, 'a king is emperor in his own realm'.

This doctrine had been developed by canon lawyers and was taken up by popes around 1200.[82] Fittingly, it was the greatest of the medieval lawyer-popes, Innocent III (r. 1198–1216), who first put his weight behind it. This happened in his 1202 decretal *Per venerabilem*, which established that a king had no other superior in secular or lay matters (whereas any king, of course, fell under the religious authority of the papacy).[83]

Innocent was the scion of a Roman noble family. After studies in Paris and Bologna, he had made a stellar rise through the church hierarchy to become cardinal around the age of 30 and reach the papal throne when he was only 37 or 38 years old. It was during his watch that the power of the papacy climaxed. Likening the Church to the sun and kingship to the moon, Innocent argued that the former was bound to outshine and illuminate the latter. In fact, using the scholastic reasoning of his day, imbibed during his university studies, Innocent offered an exact measure of papal superiority: 'Since the Earth is seven times larger than the moon, while the Sun is in turn eight times larger than the Earth, so it follows that papal dignity is fifty-seven times greater than that of a king.'[84]

Innocent not only talked the talk; he also walked the walk. He decided who would be emperor in Germany, he excommunicated rulers such as King John Lackland in England, he made both England and the Crown of Aragon papal fiefs, and he reorganised the Catholic Church itself at the Fourth Lateran Council in 1215, the greatest church meeting of the Latin West in the high Middle ages, bringing over 1,200 churchmen to Rome to settle some of the pressing questions that faced the Catholic Church.

Subsequent popes were unable to match Innocent's personality, power, prestige, and influence, but they did their best to stay the course. *Rex in regno suo imperator* was, for instance, included in the bull *Pastoralis cura*, published by Pope Clement V in 1313. It refuted the idea that the emperor lorded over kings who ruled territory not part of the empire itself. The purpose

Pope Clement V (r. 1305–1314)
Some modern scholarship has traced key norms of sovereignty back to the conflict between the papacy and lay monarchs in the High Middle Ages. In this context, the principle *rex in regno suo imperator* – "a king is emperor in his own realm" – was developed within canon law. This principle was employed by Pope Clement V, in the bull *Pastoralis cura* of 1313, which declared that a king whose territory lay outside the Holy Roman Empire was not accountable to the emperor.

was to make clear that the Angevin King Robert of Naples need not abide the commands of the newly crowned emperor, Henry VII of the House of Luxembourg. It was therefore part of the red thread of the medieval papacy: the centuries-long attempt to clip the wings of the German emperors.

The result was that what became territorial states such as France and England were able to match the empire and lay claim to a status as peers. As American medievalist Joseph R. Strayer pithily summarised this process in his book *On the Medieval Origins of the Modern State*, first published in 1970:

> [T]he claims of the revived Western Empire to universal domination could no longer be taken seriously ... Each kingdom or principality had to be treated as a separate entity; the foundations for a multi-state system had been laid.[85]

Red Beard and the Wonder of the World

The most important act in this papal onslaught against the empire dates to the period between the papacies of Innocent III and Clement V. Paradoxically, Innocent had acted as midwife of the problems that began to mount shortly after his death, and which would haunt his papal successors.

Innocent had originally supported the claim to the German throne (and hence the imperial dignity) of Otto of Brunswick of the Welf Dynasty, the main German competitor to the mighty Hohenstaufen imperial line that had held the throne since 1138, and which previous popes had struggled to keep away from their backyard in northern Italy. A famous echo of the Hohenstaufen-Welf arm-wrestling contest is found in northern Italian cities, where in the ensuing centuries, Guelphs (the Italian form of Welf) and Ghibellines (an Italianised version of the name of the Hohenstaufen castle and battle cry "*Wibellingen*") would fight vicious battles for political power. The Guelphs were normally allied with the popes, whereas the Ghibellines were followers of imperial power.

Innocent's support of Otto and the Welfs thus fit hand-in-glove with the papal balancing against imperial power. But Innocent soon found that he got more than he bargained for. Just as the papal-leaning Guelphs of Florence fell out with each other after they had vanquished the Ghibellines at the great battle of Campaldino in 1289, with internecine fighting between the White Guelphs more hostile to papal power and the Black Guelphs more aligned with it, the pope and the Welf emperor fell out when Otto attempted to assert his authority in Italy. In 1212, Innocent therefore had his ward, the young Frederick, underage ruler of Sicily and male heir of the Hohenstaufen family, elected as the German king. By the time Innocent died in 1216, Frederick's rule was uncontested.[86] But his ambitions were also limitless, and he quickly came into conflict with Innocent's papal successors.

Frederick II governed out of southern Italy as King of Sicily. To his own contemporaries he was known as *Stupor mundi*, the Wonder of the World, due to his mercurial character and as a sponsor of architecture, science and learning – he reputedly spoke six languages, including Arabic and Greek. As German king (emperor from 1220) and heir of the Hohenstaufen territories, Frederick's possessions completely encircled Rome, making the threat of a pincer movement that Innocent III had attempted to stave off by turning on Otto of Brunswick all too real.[87]

Several succeeding popes went on the offensive. Frederick was excommunicated no fewer than four times, and popes such as Gregory IX and Innocent IV allied both with the cities of northern Italy and with French royal power to keep him in check. Innocent IV even declared him *preambulus Antichristi*, forerunner of the Antichrist. The papal campaign against the Hohenstaufen family was so rancorous and self-serving that these episodes have contributed to posterity's bleak view of the medieval papacy.[88] Frederick was thus an excommunicate – officially for not honouring a pledge to take the cross – when he embarked on crusade in 1228–29 and secured control of the Holy Land through negotiations with the Ayyubid sultan of Egypt.

Frederick's fiercest and most unforgiving enemy would prove to be Pope Innocent IV, who kept up the pressure on the Hohenstaufen family after Frederick's death in 1250. Innocent and his successors excommunicated Frederick's sons, barring them from becoming emperors, and even organised a crusade against their southern Italian bastion, a campaign led by the younger brother of the French king, Charles of Anjou.

Frederick's son Manfred was defeated and killed by Charles in 1266; his grandson Conradin suffered the same fate in

1268, executed in Naples after being bested in battle. The Hohenstaufen male line had thereby been extinguished. The pope was so vindictive that he had Manfred's dead body disinterred and reburied just outside the borders of his kingdom – in a place where rain and wind would tear it, as the unfortunate Manfred would tell the Italian poet Dante Alighieri, a supporter of empire, in the *Divine Comedy*.[89]

Thus ended the great conflict between popes and the Hohenstaufen imperial family. It had begun more than a century earlier, during the reign of Frederick's namesake and grandfather Frederick I, known as Barbarossa (Red Beard) due to his hirsute appearance. The young and vigorous Frederick, crowned king in 1152 and emperor in 1155, set out to restore imperial power, which had been severely weakened by the conflict with the popes that began in the 1070s, more than 75 years earlier. Barbarossa's intention was to do this by reasserting imperial influence south of the Alps, in prosperous northern Italy, where he spent more than a third of his long reign, which lasted until 1190.[90] Imperial power had been genuine

Dante Alighieri (1265–1321)

The Italian poet and statesman Dante Alighieri became embroiled in the great medieval fight between emperors and popes. As a young man, Dante had fought on the Guelph side at Campaldino in 1289 but as member of the White Guelfs he was banished from Florence in 1302. The former Guelph was to become one of the most influential supporters of imperial power, blasting the papacy and defending empire in his political treatise *Monarchia*, written in the first quarter of the fourteenth century. The illustration shows Sandro Botticelli's famous painting of Dante.

there until the Investiture Controversy, but it had folded during the civil wars of the 1070s and 1080s, and cities such as Milan had used the power vacuum to gain autonomy.[91] Frederick Barbarossa now tried to subdue the north Italian cities, who allied with the pope and banded together in a so-called Lombard League to stave off imperial subjugation.

Shying no means, Frederick engaged in a series of bitter military campaigns to bring the northern Italian cities to heel, and back into the imperial fold. In 1162, he razed Milan, the centre of opposition against imperial rule. However, the emperor met his match in the northern Italian townsmen, who had become accustomed to political independence since the 1070s and had begun to venerate *Libertas* as something akin to a civic religion.[92]

At the Battle of Legnano on 29 May 1176, Frederick's army was bested by the Lombard forces, whose infantry managed to repel the attack of the German knights, while Lombard cavalry attacked the imperial forces from the rear. Frederick was reported missing and presumed dead, but three days later, a mangled emperor made his way to Pavia, the imperial headquarters south of the Alps, where the remains of his army had sought refuge. A truce was made with the Lombard cities, which meant that they preserved their *de facto* political autonomy while formally paying lip service to imperial authority.

The interest of the northern Italian townsmen in the conflict was clear and obvious. They were fighting for their political freedom and independence. But why did the popes engage? In a nutshell, they recognised a rival in the ambitious and assertive emperor. Barbarossa not only wanted to regain control of the imperial possessions south of the Alps but also attempted to recreate the sacral character of empire, forfeited at Worms the very same year that Frederick had been born, in 1122. It was he who added the epithet "Holy" to what would become known as the "Holy Roman Empire of the German Nation".[93] This can be seen as an attempt to turn back the clock to the time – before the humiliation at Canossa and the Concordat of Worms – where emperors had a genuine religious authority, on top of wielding the secular sword of the state.[94]

Once Bitten, Twice Shy

The great Hohenstaufen project collapsed with the death of Frederick II in 1250. What followed was a large-scale buckling of imperial power, springing from what is conventionally termed the "Great Interregnum". Until 1273, no new king was broadly recognised in Germany, as contenders such as the English earl Richard of Cornwall, younger brother of King Henry III, and the Castilian king Alfonso X cast around for support, the latter without ever setting foot on German soil. Not until 1312 was a German king again made emperor by the pope. In other words, for 92 years – from the ascension of Frederick II in 1220 to the ascension of Henry VII of the Luxembourg dynasty in 1312 – no imperial coronation occurred.[95]

The papal crowning of Henry VII in 1312 did not herald a return to the strong emperors of yore. The period after 1250 saw little in the way of the strong imperial dynasties that had

The Holy Roman Empire in the year 1000

This German map illustrates the composite territorial units and borders of the Holy Roman Empire around the year 1000. At this point, the empire was vast, encompassing substantial parts of present-day Germany, eastern France, Austria, Switzerland, and Italy. It was by far the most powerful realm in the Latin West at the time. Later emperors, such as Frederick Barbarossa (r. 1152–1190), sought to revive imperial authority in northern Italy – authority that had been forfeited during the Investiture Controversy (1075–1122).

hitherto ruled Germany. Since 919, royal dignity had descended, sequentially, in the Ottonian, Salian, and Hohenstaufen dynasties, principally changing hands when an imperial family died out in the male line. All kings/emperors with live sons had these sons crowned as co-kings during their lifetime – this happened on no fewer than eleven occasions between the mid-tenth and the mid-thirteenth century. The Great Interregnum changed this pattern. From 1254 to 1438, seven different houses claimed the title King of Germany, and in this entire period we only find one instance where the throne passed directly from father to son.[96]

The result was that imperial infrastructure went to pieces. Never again would a German ruler have the kind of imperial power that the Salians had had or that the Hohenstaufen had aspired to have. Even when the Austrian Habsburgs came to hold the imperial throne and made it *de facto* hereditary, there was no genuine revival of imperial power. By then, "empire" had in many ways become an empty shell, at least compared with the situation before the Great Interregnum. The Habsburgs were mighty due to their hereditary possessions – first in Austria and later in Bohemia, Hungary, the Low Countries, Spain, and Italy – not by virtue of having donned the purple (the colour signalling imperial dignity).[97]

The Defeat of Papal Monarchy

For a while, it seemed that the popes would try to steal the emperors' thunder. After they had broken Hohenstaufen power, several assertive popes harboured ambitions to usurp the imperial dignity. As we have seen, the self-assertive Innocent III had led the way by trying to make the papacy (the illuminating sun) the senior partner in the relationship with the empire (the illuminated moon).

But Innocent did not and probably could not imagine a world without a lay emperor. It was not until the vacant imperial throne of the Great Interregnum that the idea was broached that the pope could simply do away with the emperor. To understand this, we must factor in the normative power of empire. In late Antiquity, one of the four doctors of the Catholic Church, St Jerome, had interpreted a prophecy in the Old Testament Book of Daniel to the effect that the rise and fall of four world empires (the Babylonian or Assyrian Empire, the Persian Empire, Alexander the Great's empire, and the Roman Empire) would herald the end of time. In other words, the fall of the Holy Roman Empire – the latter-day version of the fourth and final earthly empire – would spell judgment day.

In the aftermath of the Investiture Controversy, this theory had been used by defenders of imperial power to attack the papal promotion of royal power in kingdoms such as France and England at the expense of the authority of the German emperor. Eleventh-century French monk and chronicler Rodulfus Glaber thus saw the collapse of the universal empire as heralding the coming of the Anti-Christ.[98]

These concerns further increased as a consequence of the Great Interregnum. But papal apologists were also resourceful. None other than the Dominican scholar Thomas Aquinas, in his magisterial *Summa Theologica* – written during the Great Interregnum – devised a theory to the effect that the Church now carried the torch from the Roman Empire. According to Aquinas, the Church had replaced the Holy Roman Emperors as the present-day heir to the Roman emperors of Antiquity. The empire had not disappeared after all – judgment day was postponed – despite the obvious fact that no emperor had been crowned since 1220.[99]

One is here reminded of British historian Edward Gibbon's famous remark that 'the papacy is no other than the ghost of the deceased Roman Empire, sitting crowned upon the grave thereof'. Gibbon referred to the fall of the Western Roman Empire in the fifth century, but in the thirteenth century, papal apologists directly urged the popes to claim the imperial crown. They devised what amounted to a fully-fledged theory of "papal monarchy", a fusion of lay and religious power with the pope at its centre.[100]

The attempt to implement a form of papal monarchy climaxed with Boniface VIII's (r. 1294–1303) papacy. In the absence of an emperor, Boniface fell out with the new lay strongman of the day, Capetian King of France Philip the Fair (r. 1285–1314). Boniface first tried to forbid Philip from taxing his clergy to finance war with England, to no avail. Next, a heated dispute arose as to whether the French king was allowed to correct French bishops. Boniface excommunicated Philip over the matter, and in November 1302, he issued the bull *Unam sanctam*, which declared that "outside of the Church, there is no salvation" (*Extra ecclesiam nulla salus*). This flowery phrase can be translated into something less rosy: those who resisted Boniface were resisting God Almighty, full stop.

However, Boniface had gone too far in his attempt to imitate Gregory VII's forceful policy against Henry IV two hundred years previously. Most of the French bishops sided with Philip, who sent troops to arrest the pope. Boniface was treated brutally and died in French custody in 1303. The consequence of the struggle was what Petrarch would dub the "Babylonian Captivity" of the papacy,[101] a reference to the Babylonian captivity of the Jews in the Old Testament. Between 1309 and 1376, the pope resided in Avignon, today in southern France, back then formally within the boundaries of the Holy Roman Empire but under *de facto* control of the French kings.

So, the priest did not become king after all. Both empire and papal monarchy were ultimately defeated. Power pluralism was preserved, and it became an inherent characteristic of the Latin West over time. It is time to look at the consequences.

The Consequences 5

The King-in-Parliament

On 14 May 1264, two armies faced each other outside the English town of Lewes in Sussex. One was commanded by King Henry III and his son Edward, to my generation probably best known as the Edward Longshanks of Mel Gibson's movie *Braveheart*. The other side was led by a French nobleman, Simon de Montfort, who had come to England around 1230, married into the royal family, but eventually fallen out with King Henry.

In the late 1250s, de Montfort had been one of the architects of the so-called Provisions of Oxford. This was a charter of rights the barons of the realm had forced the fickle King Henry to accept, which limited royal power in a much more radical way than the better-known Magna Carta of 1215. The Provisions also stipulated, for the first time, that what developed into the English parliament was to be recognised as a permanent political institution, which would henceforth meet thrice a year.[102]

It was Henry's refusal to live up to these provisions that sparked de Montfort's armed rebellion, supported by disgruntled barons, commercial towns, and most of the English clergy, which – they claimed – had been unlawfully taxed by King Henry.

At Lewes, the royal army outnumbered the rebels two-to-one. De Montfort's forces nonetheless prevailed, and both Henry and Edward were captured. It was therefore Simon de Montfort who, in the name of King Henry, called two celebrated meetings of the English parliament in London on 24 June 1264 and 20 January 1265. These two parliaments are famous because townsmen from a few select towns attended as representatives of their municipal councils. This was the first time townsmen attended as genuine representatives – to many historians and social scientists, the defining characteristic of medieval parliaments.[103]

King Henry – or rather his much more competent and belligerent son, Edward, who later escaped his captors – would soon turn the tables on Simon de Montfort. The very next year, Edward routed Simon's forces at Evesham. Contrary to popular depictions of medieval Europe, this was an age where rules of chivalry meant that highborn enemies were normally not executed when defeated – between 1076 and 1312 not a single English earl was murdered for political reasons.[104] But the one exception was rebels who had committed high treason (*lèse-majesté*). Edward therefore offered no quarter, and he appointed a death squad of knights to ensure that his adversary would not survive the fray; both de Montfort and his eldest son were left dead on the field of battle.

The king of England was no longer a prisoner. But he and his successors did not do away with parliamentary constraints. On the contrary, the parliament in Westminster would become an integral part of the English body politics over the next century.

It was under Edward I, the victor at Evesham, that the English 'tax-based parliamentary state'[105] was established; a state where royal power was strengthened via a successful cooperation with the local forces of the realm, meeting frequently at Westminster to grant taxes and petition the king. Among other famous parliaments, the king convened the so-called Model Parliament in 1295, with two knights from each county and two burgesses from each town as representatives. The result would be the English constitutional notion of the "king-in-parliament", which remains in force to this very day.[106]

Over the Pyrenees

The British parliamentary tradition is close to unique in Europe in one respect. As American political scientist Francis Fukuyama has observed, today's British parliament in Westminster is 'the lineal descendent of the medieval English institution of the same name'.[107] However, if we go back to the high Middle Ages, there was certainly nothing unique about the parliament that, even back then, would often meet in Westminster.

To see this, let us go further south, across France and over the Pyrenees, to the political unit known as the Crown of Aragon. The parliamentary development in this composite monarchy, bringing together the duchy of Catalonia with the kingdoms of Aragon and (later) Valencia, predates that of England. Genuine representatives of town councils were first called to attend the parliament of Lérida in August 1214. This is, to my knowledge, the first documented use of proctorial representation, based on Roman Law, at any lay medieval parliament anywhere.[108] It came directly from the papal church as the parliament – known as *cortes* in Aragonese and *corts* in Catalan – was called by the papal legate Peter of Benevento to get nobles, clergy, and townsmen to acclaim the underage James I as monarch of the Crown of Aragon. Peter of Benevento here enlisted the legal principles of representation that Innocent III, a little over a year before the Lérida assembly, in April 1213, had used to call representatives from church institutions across the Latin West to the previously mentioned Fourth Lateran Council, meeting in 1215.

The backstory is both dramatic and fascinating. James's father, Count-King Peter II of Catalonia and Aragon, had been killed at the Battle of Muret in southern France on 12 September 1213. The victor at Muret was a northern French nobleman and adventurer named Simon de Montfort, father of his namesake, the Simon de Montfort who called the English parliaments in 1264–65. De Montfort senior was leading a contingent of crusaders that Pope Innocent III had let loose on southern France to suppress the so-called Cathars, a heretical sect (in the eyes of the church hierarchy). It is from this campaign that we have a – possibly apocryphal – story about how the papal messenger Arnaud Amalric responded when asked by the crusaders how to distinguish heretical Cathars from orthodox Catholics after taking the city of Béziers in the County of Toulouse: 'Kill them [all], for God knows which are His own' (*Caedite eos. Novit enim Dominus qui sunt eius*).

King Peter had come to Muret to aid his vassals north of the Pyrenees who were threatened by the crusaders' indiscriminate violence and conquest. Indeed, matters were more intricate than this as the pope also had a stake in the Aragonese fortunes. King Peter had made the Crown of Aragon a papal fief in 1204, and Innocent was thus overlord of the now leaderless realm. He ordered Simon de Montfort to release the underage James, who had fallen into captivity after his father had been killed at Muret, and he sent a right-hand man of his, Cardinal Peter of Benevento, to sort things out in Aragon and Catalonia.[109]

Do or Die for the Crown of Aragon

The parliament at Lérida in 1214 would herald a strong parliamentary tradition, which was consolidated in the generation after the death of James I in 1276, following a long reign lasting 63 years. The backdrop of this consolidation of parliamentary power was the so-called Sicilian Vespers of 1282. This was a local uprising against King Charles of Anjou, who ruled southern Italy out of Naples with the help of French soldiers. Beginning on Easter Monday 1282 – at the time of the Vespers, the sunset prayer marking the start of the night vigil – the Sicilians massacred the French they could lay their hands on, perhaps as many as 13,000 men, women, and children, and renounced their Angevin king.

James I's son, Peter II of Aragon, seized the chance to have himself proclaimed king of Sicily, with reference to an inheritance claim of his wife Constance of Hohenstaufen, whose father Manfred had – as we have seen – ruled Sicily before being defeated and killed by Charles of Anjou in 1266. The Sicilians, fearing the wrath of Charles of Anjou and longing for the good old days when ruled by Constance's Hohenstaufen family, eagerly embraced Peter.

But the wider world was less welcoming. Charles of Anjou established a formidable coalition, consisting of his nephew, French King Philip III, French Pope Martin IV, and eventually also the Kingdom of Castile. While Charles himself would harass Sicily, the French king marched across the Alps in 1285, the campaign being blessed as a crusade by the pope.[110]

The result was a "do or die" situation for Peter and the Crown of Aragon. Peter tried to rally his troops in both Aragon and Catalonia to face the expected French onslaught. He called parliaments in both places to get them to support the war. At several Aragonese parliaments in 1283, Peter gave nobles and towns important concessions, which included strengthening the ombudsman office of the *Justicia* and promising regular convocations of the *cortes*; in Catalonia, he gave similar concessions to the *corts*. These concessions transformed the *cortes* and the *corts* from institutions called at the ruler's whim to permanent public institutions that constrained the monarch's rule.[111]

The result was what has been called the "pactist monarchy" of the Crown of Aragon, where subjects could police the monarch's power via representative institutions; a splendid cooperation between the monarch and his elite groups, much like the English "king-in-parliament". Both English and Aragonese kings discovered that institutions born to constrain their power could be used to project power. One way of understanding this is via British sociologist Michael Mann's distinction between infrastructural power, which parliaments increased, and despotic power, which they helped curtail.[112]

The Age of Parliaments and Charters of Rights

The Crown of Aragon and England were frontrunners, but similar developments took place across all of Western and Central Europe. Historians have referred to the period from 1200 to the French Revolution in 1789 as the "age of parliaments".[113] During these six centuries, European monarchs would co-rule with nobles, clergy, and townsmen – and in a few regions, members of the peasantry – via representative institutions.

Some parliaments were stronger than others. We have already seen how monarchs in the Crown of Aragon had been forced to call parliaments according to a fixed schedule, normally annually, biennially, or triennially.[114] This was certainly not the rule everywhere, and the more specific prerogatives also varied. Some parliaments had the right to declare war, to audit expenditures, to appoint royal officials, or even to elect the monarch when the old one had died – others had none of these prerogatives. However, the core function everywhere was the same: to consent to taxes needed for warfare.[115] Early in the period, European rulers were unable to tax unilaterally; they needed the consent of the groups that were to pay and collect the taxes.

Parliaments were merely the apex of a thoroughly constitutionalised political structure. Across Western and Central Europe, regional and local representative institutions were ubiquitous, as were other institutions that also had to be reckoned with by monarchs. Historians have referred to these as "intermediary institutions".[116] A good example is the *parlement* in Paris which – despite its name – was not a parliament but a court of law. However, the Paris *parlement* had the right to register royal letters and ordinances. Out of this grew the right to remonstrance: a royal law was only valid if it had been correctly registered by the *parlement*, giving its members a *de facto* veto against new laws.

This and many other intermediary institutions reflected the priority of law and rights in the exercise of power. The Magna Carta is merely the most famous of the series of charters of rights that monarchs had to grant across Western and Central Europe in the high Middle Ages. I have already mentioned the 1258 Provisions of Oxford and the constitutional concessions granted by the count-kings of Aragon in the 1280s, which include the *Privilegio General* of 1283 and the *Privilegios de la Unión* of 1287. Another famous example is the "Golden Bull" granted by Hungarian King Andrew II in 1222, which gave many of the same concessions as the Magna Carta had done seven years previously, half a continent away.

In my own native Denmark, starting with Eric V Klipping in 1282 and ending only with the introduction of absolutism in 1660, every new king had to grant a charter of rights. But it is one of the more general Danish law codes of the period, the

1241 *Jyske lov* (Code of Jutland) of King Valdemar the Victorious, that best conveys the medieval priority of law. It begins with the dictum 'With law must land be built' (*Med lov skal land bygges*), a programmatic statement for the period.

The most important functions of medieval state power concerned law and war, not taxation and administration. As Joseph Strayer has observed, European states were law states where rulers were bound morally and politically by law.[117] An earlier generation of economic historians saw this as a unique feature of medieval and early modern Europe. British-Australian economist Eric L. Jones, writing in 1981, thus claimed that 'Europe alone managed the politically remarkable feat of curtailing arbitrary power'.[118]

This is almost certainly an exaggerated view. But some aspects of the constitutional scaffolding in Europe do indeed seem unique. The practices of representation and consent via parliaments is a case in point.[119] Parliaments remain the bedrock of modern representative democracy to this day, and without the medieval development of representation and consent, it is hard to see how this regime form could ever have been devised.

The Reformation and All That

Even if readers accept this book's attempt to seek the deep origins of Europe's unique trajectory in the high Middle Ages, they will probably ask, "What about later developments?"

Fans of Max Weber are likely to object that without the Protestant Reformation, the road to the modern state, modern capitalism, and modern democracy would have remained blocked. This may or may not be the case. But it is certainly the case that the Reformation itself could not have happened in the absence of the developments set in motion by the eleventh-century Papal Revolution. The Reformation was a direct reaction against the political role popes had usurped after declaring their independence from lay power during the Gregorian reforms. And the main reason that the new heterodox protestant ideas – associated with reformers such as Martin Luther, Huldrych Zwingli, and Jean Calvin – were so hard to contain was the power pluralism of the Latin West.

The protestant movements spread like wildfire across the many self-governing towns of Western and Central Europe.[120] This fire proved so difficult to stamp out because there was no one authority of overweening power, no firefighter-general. When the Habsburg emperors – the latter-day rulers of the Holy Roman Empire – did, in fact, attempt to extinguish the Protestant blaze, they were met by countervailing forces in the form of other monarchs and strong domestic groups. In Germany, the Reformation was saved by two of the peripheral realms that Pope Gregory VII had once set out to strengthen, Denmark and Sweden, which successively intervened in the Thirty Years' War (1618–48) when the forces of the "Counterreformation" seemed on the verge of victory. The Scandinavian protestant kings were backed by Catholic

Luther nails his theses to the door of the cathedral in Wittenberg
The start of the Protestant Reformation is traditionally dated to the publication of the Ninety-five Theses, which Martin Luther is said to have nailed to the door of the Castle Church in Wittenberg in 1517. For a long time, scholars disagreed over whether this dramatic act actually took place, but more recent research suggests that Luther did indeed make his theses public in this manner. The painting is a reconstruction of the scene from 1872, *Luthers Thesenanschlag*, by the Belgian painter Ferdinand Pauwels.

France in another nod to the power pluralism that was a legacy of the eleventh-century rupture described in this little book.

These balancing dynamics would be reenacted whenever one polity made a bid for hegemony. Another peripheral state, Great Britain, would help balance France when the Sun King, Louis XIV, tried to establish a new form of European domination around 1700. A century later, the same thing happened when Napoleon Bonaparte, harnessing the popular mobilisation unleashed by the French Revolution, came perilously close to conquering all of Continental Europe. In the first half of the twentieth century, Germany made a similar bid for hegemony but this, too, was repulsed by effective balancing mechanisms. The balance of power first nurtured by medieval popes proved to have staying power.

Back to the Medieval Rubbish

But surely the Renaissance and Enlightenment criticism of things medieval has some merit? Returning to Karl Marx, was not a gigantic broom needed to clear European societies of some of the medieval rubbish – 'seignorial rights, local privileges, municipal and guild monopolies and provincial constitutions'[121] – in order to build modern states, modern democracies, and modern economies?

The answer is an unequivocal "yes". Medieval European polities were enmeshed in law, from top to bottom, and the public exercise of power was law-based. But the medieval conception of law was starkly different from our modern conception. It rested on established liberties and privileges, not the universal citizenship rights we associate with the rule of law and representative democracy today.

Privileges literally mean "private laws", laws that only apply to certain groups or even certain people and which create a fundamental inequality before the law. For instance, in many parts of Europe, the nobility and the clergy were exempt from taxation, which rather than being progressive (as it is in most democracies today) was regressive, falling on the poorer groups in society. And townsmen in self-governing towns would have other rights than those living outside the walls, including personal freedoms that downtrodden peasants could only dream about. This was one reason why serfs often fled to the towns, hoping to gain their freedom after a year and a day within the city walls.

Up until the French Revolution, the reach of these medieval privileges extended to the remotest corner of society, including most economic activities. Guilds would have monopoly rights within their professions, whether we speak of butchers, bakers, weavers, tanners, medics, or lawyers. And many nobles would have the right to force their local peasantry to bring their grain to their mills (taking a cut of the flour), and to hunt with horses in the peasants' fields, devastating the crops merely for their personal amusement. Alexis de Tocqueville has not been alone in pointing out the resentment this caused among the peasants towards the nobles.

It comes as no surprise that privileged groups fight tooth and nail to retain their special status, their private laws. In this

The February Revolution, 1848

The February Revolution in France in 1848 marked the beginning of a wave of revolutions that engulfed Western and Central Europe. In most places, the revolutionary concessions were rolled back during 1848 and 1849. The painting shows Henri Félix Emmanuel Philippoteaux's

famous depiction of the French poet and statesman Alphonse de Lamartine speaking before the Paris Town Hall on February 25, 1848, where he rejected the red, socialist flag and instead embraced the tricolor flag, first adopted during the French Revolution.

book, I have identified the privileged medieval orders as one aspect of the great internal balancing act of European state formation and, hence, a precondition for Europe's peculiar state-building trajectory. But fast-forward to the political struggles of the eighteenth, nineteenth, and twentieth centuries, and many of these groups proved the great enemies of political and economic liberty and progress, including equal and universal suffrage.

This was most obviously the case with the agrarian nobility (the great landowners), according to American sociologist Barrington Moore the enemy par excellence of modern democracy.[122] But members of guilds likewise often resisted the liberalisation of their economic activities from which they stood to lose – just as certified cab drivers do in many places today as the online economy disrupts their profession. Established political rights also worked against equal representation, illustrated by the "rotten boroughs" of Great Britain before the Reform Act of 1832. Old Sarum – a hill close to Salisbury, Wiltshire, that had been a thriving town in early Norman times – sent two MPs to Westminster until 1832 even though no-one lived there anymore! The local landowners were free to pick and choose these two MPs at their whim.

Modern democracy, the rule of law, and the market economy – in a word, modern Europe – has left these formal privileges behind. The core of the rule of law is equality before the law, modern democracy is based on equal and universal suffrage, and the hidden hand of the market only works effectively if monopolistic barriers are removed.

So, in this sense, it was indeed necessary to sweep away the medieval rubbish. This book should not be read as an attempt to belittle these monumental political struggles, where first the bourgeoisie and the farmers and later the working class repeatedly encountered determined and brutal opposition from conservative forces. It was a process where the great breakthroughs such as the American Declaration of Independence in 1776, the French Revolution in 1789, the great liberal revolutions of 1830 and 1848, and the victories of the Western democracies in 1918, 1945, and 1989 were followed by frequent – if temporary – reactions and rollbacks.

Universalising Privileges

However, this is another story that must be told elsewhere. Instead, I will end this book by hammering home the following point: the great modern political struggles for universal rights were only possible because of the power pluralism and constitutionalism that had been consolidated in the Middle Ages. This medieval baggage, to tweak Marx's metaphor, made it possible to transform European societies without discarding the notion of the state being based on law and citizenship rights. The medieval development of privileges was a precondition for the later universalisation of these rights and liberties.

Almost exactly one hundred years ago, Italian historian of ideas Guido de Ruggiero used the following image: the privileges were extended to the point where they became annulled.[123] According to de Ruggiero, the cause of this great equalisation was the very combination I have emphasised in this book: that neither the privileged social orders nor the monarchs were strong enough to unilaterally enforce their will and vision on society, writ large. The former, de Ruggiero said, would have created a small and confined political and economic elite that oppressed everyone else; the latter, a population of slaves. The persistent power pluralism was and remains the creative engine of European state formation. As American political scientist Brian M. Downing puts it:

> When Chartists marched for citizenship rights, middle classes pressed for parliamentary reforms, subjects demanded legal guarantees, and representative assemblies sought to reduce monarchical power, they were fighting new battles, but in old wars, the earlier campaigns of which had been forgotten by the new participants, as they have been by not a few social scientists.[124]

Let us stop and pause to fully take this in. The value of history is that it makes us remember; by remembering we come to understand; by understanding we come to appreciate what has made Europe special: that for a thousand years, power has begotten countervailing power, that rulers have not been unfettered, that they have not had untrammelled authority. The results of this great struggle – a twofold balance of power, within the international system and within the realm of each ruler – have often been messy and chaotic, and many Europeans living under these conditions have yearned for order, guidance, and direction. But he who will not have the messiness of divided power will get something entirely more dangerous: the despotism that Tocqueville, Orwell, and so many others have warned against. The watchword of Europe is power pluralism, and it is something that is worth fighting for, today as in the distant past.

Notes

1 Tierney (1988).
2 Marx (1968, 289).
3 Hintze (1975[1906]); Hintze, (1975[1931]).
4 Waltz 1959[1954]; Waltz (1979).
5 Duby (1980); see also Poggi (1978); Finer (1997).
6 Gellner (1994).
7 de Tocqueville (1984[1835/1840]); de Tocqueville (1955[1856]).
8 Mills (1959, 152–3); Skocpol (1984, 1); Goldstone (1998, 250); Pomeranz (2000, 3).
9 Chirot (1985); Hall (2001); Mitterauer (2010).
10 Bosker, Buringh, and van Zanden (2013, 1424); Stasavage (2016, 152–53); Stasavage 2020; Wickham (2016, 136, 217).
11 Pomeranz (2000).
12 See also Stasavage (2016); Stasavage (2020).
13 Berman (1983, 15–19).
14 Møller and Doucette (2022); Grzymala-Busse (2023).
15 Hintze, (1975[1931]); see also Hintze (1962[1929]); Hintze (1962[1930]).
16 Robinson (2019); Stasavage (2020).
17 Southern (1956, 19–20); Wickham (2009, 430, 523); Wickham (2016, 64, 77).
18 Scheidel (2019).
19 Hui (2004); Hui (2005). See also Parker (1996[1988], 1–4).
20 Dincecco and Wang (2018, 346).
21 Finer (1996; 1997); Wong (1997). To quote one of Finer's (1996, 179) observations: 'The "high" period of Egyptian government and administration really lasted 1520–c.1150 BC ... For any comparison we must turn to China, where the Han Empire lasted some four centuries with only a brief interval of usurpation and civil war between AD 9 and 23. Neither Persia nor Rome nor Byzantium could show such stability over so long a period.'
22 Finer (1997, 1473).
23 See Wickham (2015a).
24 See Southern (1970); Oakley (2010).
25 Oakley (2012, 41). See also Tierney (1988, 1–2).
26 Oakley (2015, 128).
27 Gellner (1988, 94).
28 See Finer (1996); Finer (1997).
29 Tierney (1988, 1–2).
30 This section is mainly based on the description in Cowdrey (1998, Chapter 3). See also Jordan (2001); Wickham (2009); Wickham (2016).
31 The phrase 'false monk' was only used later by Henry, namely at the synod of Brixen in 1080 (see Cowdrey 1998, 201).
32 Bartlett (2020, 417).
33 Cowdrey (1998, 231).
34 (2006, 64–72). This section is based more generally on Doucette and Møller (2024).
35 Tyerman (2011, 185).
36 Riley-Smith (2008, 32).
37 See, e.g., Tyerman (2006, 248); Riley-Smith (1997, 77).
38 Tyerman (2006, 172).
39 (2000, 271); Jordan (2001, 88–91); Wickham (2015b, 24–25); Wickham (2016, 112); Wilson (2016, 54).
40 Cowdrey (1998, 68–70; 281–86).
41 Cowdrey (1998, 502–7).
42 Tierney (1988, 86); Ullmann (1970 [1955], 296); Wilson (2016, 89–90).
43 Whaley (2018, 27).
44 Quoted in Carpenter (2003, 209).
45 See Southern (1970, 37–89, Jordan (2001, 99); Wilson (2016, 60–1). On the Kingdom of England, see Gillingham and Griffiths (2000 [1984], 15).
46 Oakley (2012, 37); Oakley (2015, 4).
47 Gillingham and Griffiths (2000 [1984], 25).
48 Southern (1970, 96).
49 Cowdrey (1998, 5). See also Wickham (2009, 172); Oakley (2010, 215). For a fuller, balanced description, see Wickham (2015a).

50 Oakley (2010, 218).
51 Wickham (2015a, 453).
52 Cowdrey (1998, 21–22).
53 Ullmann (1970[1955], 251–52).
54 See Cowdrey (1998, 242).
55 Morris (1989, 33, 80); Oakley (2010, 220–21); Jasper (2012, 440, 444).
56 Cowdrey (1970, 46); Moore (2000, 5); Wickham (2016, 112).
57 Wilson (2016, 52–54, 513); Cowdrey (2000, 271).
58 Moore (1985, 77).
59 See Cowdrey (1998, 128, 281–6); Wickham (2015b, 24–25).
60 Ullmann (1970[1955], 251–52); Moore (1985, 54); Cowdrey (1998, Chapter 1).
61 Cowdrey (1998, 80).
62 Ullmann (1970[1955], 298); Tierney (1988, 36); Cowdrey (1998, 44).
63 Morris (1989, 106).
64 Cowdrey (1998, 546–47, 690).
65 Moore (1985, 54–55); Cowdrey (1998, 119–20); Wickham (2016, 114).
66 Cowdrey (1998, 272).
67 Cowdrey (1998, 75).
68 Cowdrey (1998, Chapter 5); Jordan (2001, 52–62); Wickham (2016, 102).
69 Bouchard (1987, 129).
70 Moore (2000, 28, 133); Bisson (2009, 220–21); Wickham (2016, 106–7, 112). For a more general analysis, see Doucette and Møller (2021).
71 Wickham (2016, 116).
72 Bartlett (1993, 311).
73 Cowdrey (1998, 47, 427–34).
74 Riley-Smith (1997, 44–46). For a general analysis, see Doucette and Møller (2024).
75 Riley-Smith (1997, 106–7).
76 Cowdrey (1998, 443–48, 550).
77 Cowdrey (1998, 620–28).
78 Cowdrey (1998, 424).
79 Cowdrey (1998, 424).
80 Cowdrey (1998, 550).
81 For a general analysis, see Møller and Doucette (2022: Chapter 4).
82 Fried (2015, 272).
83 Black (1992, 113).
84 Fried (2015, 239).
85 Strayer (1970, 22, 23).
86 Wilson (2016, 64–66, 355–78).
87 Wilson (2016, 64–66).
88 Møller and Doucette (2022, 148–50).
89 Bartlett (2020, 279–80).
90 Bartlett (2020, 417).
91 For a general analysis, see Wickham (2015b).
92 Whaley (2018, 53); Wilson (2016, 355–78).
93 Jordan (2001, 147–48).
94 See Oakley (2010; 2012).
95 Bartlett (2020, 399).
96 Bartlett (2020, 398).
97 See Wilson (2016); Whaley (2018).
98 Wilson (2016, 39–41).
99 Osiander (2007, 282).
100 Tierney (1988, 152–53).
101 See Møller and Doucette (2022, 135–37).
102 Maddicott (1996, 158, 352); Carpenter (1999, 338); Maddicott (2010, 234–38).
103 Møller and Doucette (2022, 93–96).
104 Carpenter (2003, 127).
105 Carpenter (2003, 466).
106 See Stasavage (2020, 101–37).
107 Fukuyama (2015, 125).
108 See Møller (2018).
109 Kagay (1981, 68).
110 Kagay (1981, 213).
111 For a close description, see Kagay (1981); Møller and Doucette (2022, 167–70); see also Bisson (1986).
112 Mann (1986, Chapter 1).
113 The following section builds on Myers (1975).
114 See Møller (2017).
115 Stasavage (2010).
116 See Finer (1997, Chapter 8).
117 See Strayer (1970); see also Fukuyama (2011).
118 Jones (2003[1981], xiv).
119 Stasavage (2016); but see Stasavage (2020).
120 Becker, Pfaff, and Rubin (2016).
121 Marx (1968, 289).
122 Moore (1991[1966]).
123 de Ruggiero (1927, 4).
124 Downing (1992, 18).

Bibliography

Acemoğlu, Daron and James A. Robinson (2019). *The Narrow Corridor: States, Societies, and the Fate of Liberty*. New York: Penguin Press.

Bartlett, Robert (1993). *The Making of Europe: Conquest, Colonization and Cultural Change 950–1350*. Princeton University Press.

Bartlett, Robert (2020). *Blood Royal: Dynastic Politics in Medieval Europe*. Cambridge: Cambridge University Press

Becker, Sascha, Steven Pfaff, and Jared Rubin (2016). 'Causes and Consequences of the Protestant Reformation'. *Explorations in Economic History* 62, 1–25.

Berman, Harold J. (1983). *Law and Revolution: The Formation of the Western Legal Tradition*. Cambridge: Harvard University Press.

Bisson, Thomas N. (1986). *The Medieval Crown of Aragon: A Short History*. Oxford: Clarendon Press.

Bisson, Thomas N. (2009). *The Crisis of the Twelfth Century: Power, Lordship, and the Origins of European Government*. New Haven: Princeton University Press.

Black, Antony (1992). *Political Thought in Europe 1250–1450*. Cambridge: Cambridge University Press.

Bosker, Maarten, Eltjo Buringh and Jan Luiten van Zanden (2013). 'From Baghdad to London: Unravelling Urban Development in Europe and the Arab World 800–1800'. *Review of Economics and Statistics* 95 (4), 1418–37.

Bouchard, Constance (1987). *Sword, Miter, and Cloister: Nobility and the Church in Burgundy, 990–1198*. Ithaca: Cornell University Press.

Carpenter, David A. (1999). 'The Plantagenet Kings', in Abulafia, David (ed.). *The New Cambridge Medieval History: c.1198-c.1300*. Cambridge: Cambridge University Press.

Carpenter, David A. (2003). *The Struggle for Mastery: The Penguin History of Britain 1066–1284*. London: Penguin.

Chirot, D. (1985). 'The Rise of the West'. *American Sociological Review* 50 (2), 181–95.

Cowdrey, Herbert Edward John (1970). 'The Peace and the Truce of God in the Eleventh Century'. *Past & Present* 46, 42–67.

Cowdrey, Herbert Edward John (1998). *Pope Gregory VII, 1073–1085*. Oxford: Oxford University Press.

Cowdrey, Herbert Edward John (2000). *Popes and Church Reform in the 11th Century*. London: Ashgate.

Dincecco, Mark, and Yuhua Wang (2018). 'Violent Conflict and Political Development over the Long Run: China versus Europe'. *Annual Review of Political Science* 21, 341–58.

Doucette, Jonathan Stavnskær and Jørgen Møller (2021). 'The Collapse of State Power, the Cluniac Reform Movement, and the Origins of Urban Self-Government in Medieval Europe'. *International Organization* 75 (1), 204–23.

Doucette, Jonathan Stavnskær and Jørgen Møller (2024). 'The Christianization of War: How the Church Reform Movement Incentivized Armsbearing Elites to Conquer the Holy Land'. *Journal of Historical Political Economy* 4 (2), 189–219.

Downing, Brian M. (1992). *The Military Revolution and Political Change: Origins of Democracy and Autocracy in Early Modern Europe*. Princeton: Princeton University Press.

Duby, Georges (1980). *The Three Orders: Feudal Society Imagined*. Chicago: University of Chicago Press.

Finer, Samuel E. (1996). *The History of Government I. Ancient Monarchies and Empires*. Oxford: Oxford University Press.

Finer, Samuel E. (1997). *The History of Government II. The Intermediate Ages*. Oxford: Oxford University Press.

Fried, Johannes (2015). *The Middle Ages*. Cambridge: Harvard University Press.

Fukuyama, Francis (2011). *The Origins of Political Order: From Prehuman Times to the French Revolution*. London: Profile Books.

Fukuyama, Francis (2015). 'Comment on Møller: The Importance of Equality'. *Journal of Democracy* 26 (3), 124–28.

Gellner, Ernest (1988). *Plough, Sword, and Book: The Structure of Human History*. Chicago: University of Chicago Press.

Gellner, Ernest (1994). *Conditions of Liberty: Civil Society and Its Rivals*. London: Hamish Hamilton.

Gillingham, John and Ralph A. Griffiths (2000 [1984]). *Medieval Britain: A Very Short Introduction*. Oxford: Oxford University Press.

Goldstone, John A. (1998). 'The Problem of the 'Early Modern' World'. *Journal of the Economic and Social History of the Orient* 41 (3), 249–84.

Grzymala-Busse, Anna (2023). *Sacred Foundations: The Medieval and Religious Roots of European State Formation*. New Haven: Princeton University Press.

Hall, John A. (2001). 'Confessions of a Eurocentric'. *International Sociology* 16 (3), 488–97.

Hintze, Otto (1975[1906]). 'Military Organization and the Organization of the State', in *The Historical Essays of Otto Hintze*. New York: Oxford University Press.

Hintze, Otto (1962[1929]). 'Wesen und Verbreitung des Feudalismus', in *Staat und Verfassung*, Vol. 1. Göttingen: Vandenhoeck & Ruprecht.

Hintze, Otto (1962[1930]). 'Typologie der ständischen Verfassungen des Abenlandes', in *Staat und Verfassung*, Vol. 1. Göttingen: Vandenhoeck & Ruprecht.

Hintze, Otto (1975[1931]). 'The Preconditions of Representative Government in the Context of World History', in *The Historical Essays of Otto Hintze*. New York: Oxford University Press.

Hui, Victoria T. (2004). 'Toward a Dynamic Theory of International Politics: Insights from Comparing the Ancient Chinese and Early Modern European Systems'. *International Organization* 58 (1), 175–205.

Hui, Victoria T. (2005). *War and State Formation in Ancient China and Early Modern Europe*. Cambridge: Cambridge University Press.

Jasper, Kathryn L. (2012). 'The Economics of Reform in the Middle Ages'. *History Compass* 10 (6), 440–54.

Jones, Eric L. (2003[1981]). *The European Miracle. Environments, Economies and Geopolitics in the History of Europe and Asia*. Cambridge: Cambridge University Press.

Jordan, William Chester (2001). *Europe in the High Middle Ages*. London: Penguin.

Kagay, Donald J. (1981). *The Development of the Cortes in the Crown of Aragon, 1064–1327*. ETD Collection for Fordham University.

Maddicott, John R. (1996). *Simon de Montfort*. Cambridge: Cambridge University Press.

Maddicott, John R. (2010). *The Origins of the English Parliament, 924–1327*. Oxford: Oxford University Press.

Mann, Michael (1986). *The Sources of Social Power: A History of Power from the Beginning to AD 1760*. Cambridge: Cambridge University Press.

Marx, Karl (1968). 'The Civil War in France', in Marx, Karl and Frederick Engels, *Selected Works in One Volume*. New York: International Publishers.

Mills, Charles Wright (1959). *The Sociological Imagination*. Oxford: Oxford University Press.

Mitterauer, Michael (2010). *Why Europe?: The Medieval Origins of its Special Path*. Chicago: University of Chicago Press.

Moore, B. (1991[1966]). *Social Origins of Dictatorship and Democracy: Lord and Peasant in the Making of the Modern World*. London: Penguin.

Moore, Robert I. (1985). *The Origins of European Dissent*. Oxford: Basil Blackwell.

Moore, Robert I. (2000). *The First European Revolution, c. 970–1215*. Blackwell.

Morris, Colin (1989). *The Papal Monarchy: The Western Church from 1050 to 1250*. Clarendon Press.

Myers, A.R. (1975). *Parliaments and Estates in Europe to 1789*. London: Thames and Hudson.

Møller, Jørgen (2017). 'The Birth of Representative Institutions: The Case of the Crown of Aragon'. *Social Science History* 41(2), 175–200.

Møller, Jørgen (2018). 'The Ecclesiastical Roots of Representation and Consent', *Perspectives on Politics* 16 (4), 1075–86.

Møller, Jørgen and Jonathan Stavnskær Doucette (2022). *The Catholic Church and European State Formation, AD 1000–1500*. Oxford: Oxford University Press.

Oakley, Francis (2010). *Empty Bottles of Gentilism: Kingship and the Divine in Late Antiquity and the Early Middle Ages (to 1050)*. New Haven and London: Yale University Press.

Oakley, Francis (2012). *The Mortgage of the Past: Reshaping the Ancient Political Inheritance (1050–1300)*. New Haven and London: Yale University Press.

Oakley, Francis (2015). *The Watershed of Modern Politics: Law, Virtue, Kingship, and Consent (1300–1650)*. New Haven and London: Yale University Press.

Osiander, Andreas (2007). *Before the State: Systemic Political Change in the West from the Greeks to the French Revolution*. Oxford: Oxford University Press.

Parker, Geoffrey (1996[1988]). *The Military Revolution: Military Innovation and the Rise of the West, 1500–1800*. Cambridge: Cambridge University Press.

Poggi, Gianfranco (1978). *The Development of the Modern State: A Sociological Introduction*. Stanford: Stanford University Press.

Pomeranz, Kenneth (2000). *The Great Divergence: Europe, China, and the Making of the Modern World Economy*. Princeton, NJ: Princeton University Press.

Riley-Smith, Jonathan (1997). *The First Crusades: 1095–1131*. Cambridge: CUP.

Riley-Smith, Jonathan (2005[1987]). *The Crusades: A History*. London: Continuum.

Riley-Smith, Jonathan (2008). *The Crusades, Christianity, and Islam*. New York: Columbia University Press.

Ruggiero, Guido de (1927). *The History of European Liberalism*, Beacon Press, Boston.

Scheidel, Walter (2019). *Escape from Rome: The Failure of Empire and the Road to Prosperity*. Princeton: Princeton University Press.

Skocpol, Theda (1984). 'Sociology's Historical Imagination', in Skocpol, Theda (ed.) *Vision and Method in Historical Sociology*. Cambridge: Cambridge University Press, 1–21.

Southern, Richard W. (1956). *The Making of the Middle Ages*. London: Hutchinson & Co.

Southern, Richard W. (1970). *Western Society and the Church in the Middle Ages*. New York: Penguin Books.

Stasavage, David (2010). 'When Distance Mattered: Geographic Scale and the Development of European Representative Assemblies'. *American Political Science Review* 104 (4), 625–43.

Stasavage, David (2016). 'Representation and Consent: Why They Arose in Europe and Not Elsewhere'. *Annual Review of Political Science* 19, 145–62.

Stasavage, David (2020). *The Decline and Rise of Democracy*. New Haven: Princeton University Press.

Strayer, Joseph R. (1970). *On the Medieval Origins of the Modern State*. Princeton, NJ: Princeton University Press.

Tierney, Brian (1988). *The Crisis of Church and State, 1050–1300*. Toronto: University of Toronto Press.

de Tocqueville, Alexis (1984[1835/1840]). *Democracy in America*. New York: Penguin Books.

de Tocqueville, Alexis (1955[1856]). *The Old Régime and the French Revolution*. New York: Doubleday Anchor Books.

Tyerman, Christopher (2006). *God's War: A New History of the Crusades*. Cambridge: Harvard University Press.

Tyerman, Christopher (2011). *The Debate on the Crusades, 1099–2010*. Manchester: Manchester University Press.

Ullmann, Walter (1970[1955]). *The Growth of Papal Government in the Middle Ages*. London: Methuen & Co. Ltd.

Waltz, Kenneth N. (1959[1954]). *Man, the State, and War: A Theoretical Analysis*. New York: Columbia University Press.

Waltz, Kenneth N. (1979). *Theory of International Politics*. Reading, MA: Addison-Wesley.

Whaley, Joachim (2018). *The Holy Roman Empire: A Very Short Introduction*. Oxford: Oxford University Press.

Wickham, Chris (2009). *The Inheritance of Rome: A History of Europe from 400 to 1000*. London: Penguin Books.

Wickham, Chris (2015a). *Medieval Rome: Stability & Crisis of a City, 900–1150*. Oxford: Oxford University Press.

Wickham, Chris (2015b). *Sleepwalking into a New World: The Emergence of Italian City Communes in the Twelfth Century*. New Haven: Princeton University Press.

Wickham, Chris (2016). *Medieval Europe: From the Breakup of the Western Roman Empire to the Reformation*. New Haven: Yale University Press.

Wilson, Peter (2016). *Heart of Europe: A History of the Holy Roman Empire*. Cambridge: Harvard University Press.

Wong, Roy Bin (1997). *China Transformed: Historical Change and the Limits of European Experience*. Ithaca, London: Cornell University Press.

Credits

Chapter 1. The Claim

Max Weber, 1918. Wikimedia Commons, Public Domain

Chapter 2. The Rupture

The Arch of Constantine, 2022. Wikimedia Commons, CC BY-SA 4.0

Henry's Walk to Canossa, 1862. Eduard Schwoiser (1826–1902), Wikimedia Commons, Public Domain

The Concordat of Worms, Mainz 1125. Alamy.com

Chapter 3. The Backdrop

Reconstructed Model of Cluny Abbey, 1887–1901. Georg Dehio/ Gustav von Bezold: *Kirchliche Baukunst des Abendlandes*. Stuttgart: Verlag der Cotta'schen Buchhandlung 1887–1901, Plate No. 212. Wikimedia Commons, Public Domain

The Tripartition of the Frankish Empire at Verdun, 843. Histoire Et Géographie – Atlas Général Vidal-Lablache, Librairie Armand Colin, Paris, 1898. Wikimedia Commons, Public Domain

Hagia Sophia, 2020. Wikimedia Commons, CC BY-SA 4.0

Chapter 4. The Measures

Pope Clement V (r. 1305–1314), 1313. Wikimedia Commons, CC BY 3.0

Dante Alighieri, circa 1495. Sandro Botticelli (1445–1510), Wikimedia Commons, Public Domain

The Holy Roman Empire in the year 1000, 2012. Wikimedia Commons

Chapter 5. The Consequences

Luther nails his theses to the door of the cathedral in Wittenberg, 1872. Ferdinand Pauwels (1830–1904), Alamy.com

The February Revolution, 1848. Henri Félix Emmanuel Philippoteaux (1815–1884), Wikimedia Commons, Public Domain

Why Europe?

Cover, layout and typesetting:
Carl-H.K. Zakrisson and Tod Alan Spoerl
Cover illustration: Heinrich Bünting (1545–1606):
"Die gantze Welt in einem Kleberblat / Welches ist der
Stadt Hannover meines lieben Vaterlandes Wapen" (1581),
Wikimedia Commons
Publishing editor: Henrik Jensen
This book is typeset in Kaius

1st edition, 1st impression

ISBN 978 87 7597 001 8 (printed book)
ISBN 978 87 7645 104 2 (e-pdf)
ISBN 978 87 7645 105 9 (epub)

Aarhus University Press
Helsingforsgade 25, DK–8200 Aarhus N
unipress@unipress.au.dk
aarhusuniversitypress.dk

Published with the financial support of
Aarhus University Research Foundation

PEER
REVIEWED

www.ingramcontent.com/pod-product-compliance
Lightning Source LLC
LaVergne TN
LVHW052307100826
845147LV00006B/693